This personal essay by Chaja Polak was written shortly after the Hamas attacks on Israel on 7 October 2023.

'Literature is one way to bridge a gap, an attempt at contributing to an understanding of the Other. An essay (the word was coined by Montaigne) is longer than an article, shorter than a book. It seeks to reach a wide audience and is characterized by a passionate and serious personal style.

The author's motivation is curiosity, to discover something about oneself related to the subject, and the human condition, how we function in certain circumstances, whether it be emotionally, intellectually or socially. Montaigne took his long thoughts for a short walk, writing in an outrageously frank and radically honest way.'
— *The Publisher*

'This long essay is skillful in its language, evocative, and difficult. Rightly so, because the problems she confronts are themselves so difficult. In presenting a vortex of citations, qualifications, attempts at moderation, this Dutch child Holocaust survivor's composition prioritises distress over clear reasoning. In short, it is a sad and faithful reflection on and of the current Jewish condition.'
— *Michael Pinto-Duschinsky, Holocaust child survivor and eminent political scientist*, London and Oxford, 2025

'Very strong, well balanced and passionate.'
— *Michael Ignatieff, historian and author of* On Consolation: Finding Solace in Dark Times, *2021*

Chaja Polak

A Letter in the Night

Reflections on Israel and Gaza

TRANSLATED by Astrid Alben

The New Menard Press

'Car nous voulons la Nuance encor,
Pas la Couleur, rien que la nuance!'
— *Paul Verlaine, 'Art poétique'*

For Rens, Anne-Sara, Jikke and Chajale

I

As I write the first sentences of this essay, bombs fall on Gaza, rockets fall on Israel; October 7, the day the world started to come apart at the seams, is behind us, four unsuspecting Hanukkah lights burn on the table in my room, my family in Israel is begging for a miracle, and I keep thinking about an article in Haaretz—a leftwing Israeli newspaper read by only five percent of the population—I keep thinking about an article that won't let me go.

It tells the story of Yuval Abraham and Ahmed Alnaouq, both journalists, one from Israel, the other from Gaza. Two young men, still in their twenties. Both convinced that peace is most likely to be brought about through mutual learning and understanding the 'enemy', the 'Other'. In 2019, they launched a plan: Palestinians from Gaza were invited to write letters about their daily lives, their worries and concerns, their hopes and desires. These digital letters would be published under the title 'Across the Wall' on an Israeli website and were meant for Israeli eyes. And hearts. No sooner than the project had been announced on Facebook, a hundred and fifty Israelis offered to translate the letters from Arabic into Hebrew. And so, this humble project came to be. The letters offered a glimpse of that dark unknown strip of overpopulated land, letting in light and air. It wasn't just everyday concerns that people wrote about, for poverty and dictatorship once more held sway over that narrow strip of land, and yet, through the crack of light created by words and sentences—by language—ordinary people were revealed to be living there, people who in their spare time enjoyed going out with family and friends— to the seaside, to the beach, to the park. People who celebrated birthdays and worried about, or were proud of, their children's grades at school. People who fell in love, got married, cooked dinner and put their children to bed. These letters transformed Gazans, in the eyes of Israelis, from hostile neighbours boxed in by high walls and barbed-wire fences, into people they could recognise.

They had met each other, these two journalists. I imagine somewhere in Europe, possibly at a conference. They struck up a conversation; by chance they found themselves at the same table adorned with pamphlets and books, or they had stood in line for the cloakroom at the same time. They struck up a conversation, soon surprised by the mutual recognition of their worries, by their shared dreams. They put on their coats and decided to continue their conversation in a café. I imagine them sitting across from each other at a brown wooden cafe table; they are drinking black coffee with lots of sugar, and while they talk, their lean, heated faces move closer together across the table. It is four years before 7 October 2023. The young men look like each other, their resemblance obvious to the other guests in the café. Both have dark hair, dark eyes under dark eyebrows, one of them with several days of beard growth. Their clothes are washed out, their voices whisper hoarsely. They must be brothers, the guests think. Or cousins.

In my imagination, this is where their plan of hope was hatched, right there in that café.

Across the Wall, translated by Israelis, is read for a number of years. Sometimes with an open mind, sometimes reluctantly, but it was read, and, tentatively, more and more people from both countries took part in the project. That is, until 7 October, the day of the sadistic bloodbath by Hamas. With more than twelve hundred dead and two hundred and thirty hostages. Predominantly young, left-wing peace activists.

Then the world came apart at the seams.

The letter exchange project now hangs suspended over Israel and Gaza, lost between the bombs and rockets, high in the digital sky.

And it hurts to know that, as *Foreign Affairs* (an American magazine for in-depth analysis and debate of foreign policy) reported on 25 October 2023, that in the period prior to the attack a large majority of Gazans were frustrated with the Hamas leadership and did not support its ideology.

On that 7th of October, and in the weeks that followed, Ahmed Alnaouq, the Gazan journalist, found himself somewhere in England. I assume in London. He cannot go back. Racked with worry at the alarming reports coming out of his homeland, he wants nothing more than to go to his family. But the borders were closed to him. It was then that Alnaouq received the news that almost his entire family, twenty-one people, lay buried under the rubble of their home. The peace project of the two inspired journalists came to an abrupt end. An end also, perhaps, to their friendship.

I picture the young Palestinian from Gaza wandering the streets of London, evening falling, night falling, as he walks and walks. He is trying to make some sort of sense of the death of his family. "I am alone", he must have uttered with every step, alone. My parents are no longer there, my grandparents are no longer there, and my sisters and brothers and their young families, they are no longer there, I am alone. It gets light again, the day breaks, and he walks and walks.

II

How familiar this uprootedness is to me. I spent happy years with my second husband, whose family was murdered in the Second World War. He no longer had grandparents, parents, all four brothers on his father's side and their young families had been murdered. And he, my husband Nol van Dijk, then a fourteen-year-old boy, had to continue with his life after the Nazis had been defeated and the peace treaties signed. A child of just fourteen years of age. Only his little sister and his mother's youngest brother had 'returned'. Of the larger van Dijk family and the smaller Mouwes family, just three splinters had survived.

The fourteen-year-old boy hid his grief in a small but sturdy box; he hid it under his skin, somewhere at the height of his stomach. That's how he talked about it. He said he had slammed the lid shut. The grief stowed away and gone. His parents, too, were in that box: also gone. Even though he was already eleven when his mother had torn the Star of David off his little cardigan, and that of his young sister's, and both children walked out of their street, without their stars and held by the hand by strange 'uncles', he had 'forgotten' them. His little sister had turned around and waved. But the boy had not looked back, had not waved to his father and mother as they watched on, half-hidden, from behind the curtains in front of the window, as their children walked down the street, turned the corner and disappeared from view forever.

Memories of his parents had been erased from my husband's memory. Memories of the house he grew up in, yes, he did have those, crystal clear pictures of the rooms, of the stairs leading up to the first and second floors, and from there to the attic. He remembered the hatch in the ceiling to the loft space and how only he, balancing on the bannister, could hoist himself up by his young boy's arms and crawl inside.

Where he loved to play, in his den. And where, when the war broke out, he hid some copper objects and a photo album at his parents' request. He could remember that exactly, but the rooms in his memory remained bare and uninhabited, as did the kitchen, as did the bedrooms. And the garden, in his memory, lay deserted.

He could not recall his father, nor his mother, although he was already eleven years old when he was separated from them. He did not know why, it was just something he'd observed.

Only a few days before his death did the insight break through. It is difficult for me to write about this, but I will force myself and I know that Nol would approve. Tell them, he would even have said. Let them know. And so I shall.

We had just heard that he would not get better, weakened and emaciated he sat in his armchair. It was silent in the house. Friends who had come to say farewell had just left. He said my name. I stood in the room, he sat. We looked at each other, and then he said: "Then I would have had to see them die in the gas chambers."

The question of guilt. A senseless question, but still, I can't help but ask it. The guilt of my husband's family was 'that they were Jews'. The guilt of the six million Jewish dead was that they were Jews. But where lay the guilt of the Palestinian family of our idealistic journalist? Were they guilty because they were Palestinians?

Hamas is guilty of its fanatical religious-political struggle aimed at destroying Israel, aimed at stifling any criticism from its own citizens, Hamas is guilty of its dictatorial and intolerant policies; the ups and downs of its own people leave Hamas unmoved.

The extremist government of Netanyahu is guilty because it deliberately allowed Hamas' power to grow and, in this way, sowed discord between Hamas and the more moderate Fatah, led by Mahmoud Abbas: a contemptible divide-and-conquer policy. The Netanyahu government is guilty because it is occupying another nation and depriving another people of its freedom, as David Grossman ceaselessly warns us. Through this occupation, the author says, Israel is denying the humanity of the other. The colonists on the West Bank are guilty for occupying Palestinian land and laying siege to its inhabitants. And the world that stayed silent and turned away indifferently, it too is guilty.

Now Palestinian citizens are paying with their lives for Hamas's guilt and the guilt of Netanyahu's government and that of the indifference of world leaders. Israeli citizens and Jews worldwide, too, are paying the price for the bankruptcy of their safety.

III

The journalist from Gaza is an adult, too old to be able to wipe his parents' faces from his memory. Too old to hide his parents and grandparents and his extended family members in a box, slam the lid shut and hide it under his skin, at the level of his stomach. As my husband did when he was a child. Although, sometimes the lid cracked open. When he was too weak to hold it tightly shut. Due to illness, or feeling displaced in an unfamiliar bed, wherever that may be, in his own country or abroad. Because an unfamiliar bed could unintentionally transport him back to the day when those two 'strange uncles' led him by the hand out of the street of his childhood and he did not wave to his father and mother, but continued to stare straight ahead, and boarded a tram with the uncles and after that a train and another train and finally a bus, and to see, at the end of that long day, an unfamiliar door open to an unfamiliar house, and led by his uncle's hands, step into a corridor where it smelled strange and so differently than at home, and where not much later he was put to bed in an unfamiliar bed, in an unfamiliar room, homesick and alone. Again and again, throughout his life, at the start of a trip to a holiday cottage, to a hotel, that memory, that trauma would push the lid open—it would take a night and a day to close the lid again, the trauma back inside.

The journalist from Gaza, Ahmed Alnaouq, has no such box with which to protect himself from his grief; he was an adult when he lost his family. In truth, Nol's 'hiding ability' was questionable too. The lid was indeed closed, but sorrow seeped out like smoke from the small box and infiltrated his thoughts, his feelings. What helped against that was humour, lots of humour. What helped was generosity. What also helped was understanding for truly everyone. And a positive outlook on life. And a lot of love for his children and grandchildren. And for my children and grandchildren, and for me. What helped was not knowing what, ultimately, he did know, something that only became clear to him a few days before he died. But he never was able to retrieve the faces of his parents from the past.

The journalist from Gaza is besieged by visions. He sees his family trapped underneath the rubble, he guesses their last thoughts, he wonders how long it took for them to die and fervently hopes that they were killed instantly. A blow, a shock, and gone. He fears that it did not happen in that way, even if he wishes it did. He sees their bodies buried under the rubble, hears their familiar voices calling for help, hears their voices fading. Until they fall silent and there is only silence. He fights against these images. He doesn't want to see them, but he sees them.

My husband and the journalist, how well they would have understood each other. They would not have had to explain anything, not a word, not an image, nor even the holding back of tears. Not even anger, probably. The journalist will never know how long it took for his family to die. The little boy who became my husband knew exactly how long it took for his parents to die from suffocation in the gas chamber; it took twenty minutes, sometimes a little longer.

IV

Life with my second husband brought plenty of the joys of mutual recognition. Our family albums, for example, turned out to be pretty much interchangeable. Our families lived, without ever crossing paths, by the way, in The Hague and Scheveningen. There are countless snapshots at the beach: short people, both his family and mine, with dark hair and dark eyes. The same wicker deckchairs, the same happy faces, the women in oversized, dark swimming costumes; and sand, lots and lots of sand, sea and sunshine. These must have been summer days packed with carefree joy, though Nazi Germany already growled at the border.

My husband recovered his family photo album from the loft in his childhood home in Scheveningen. After the war, he had gone there with his mother's youngest brother, Uncle Lou. They stood in front of the door for which they no longer had the key. Nol rang his own front door bell and waited. They waited until someone opened the door. Someone now living there. "Might the young lad take a look in the loft?", Uncle Lou had asked. He could. But the boy was no longer as small as he had been when he lived there with his parents and little sister. More than two and a half years had passed. He had grown too tall for the acrobatics he used to perform, balancing on the railing at the top of the stairwell, pulling himself up by his arms, vanishing through the opening into the loft. Uncle Lou and Nol had to borrow a ladder from the butcher on the corner, opposite the boy's home. Was this at the suggestion of the residents of the home of his childhood, did they say, just go to the butcher, he has many of your things, perhaps also the ladder? However it came about, Uncle Lou and the boy walked out the door again and stepped into the butcher shop with the request to borrow a ladder. They could. The butcher, who must have recognised Nol, didn't flinch.

The ladder turned out to be indeed Nol's parents' old ladder. There they went, again, Uncle Lou and the boy, they crossed the street, back to the parental home. The very house that Nol's paternal grandfather, Van Dijk Senior, had bought for his youngest son and daughter-in-law.

Climbing the stepladder, Nol managed to squeeze into 'his den', from where he retrieved some copper artefacts, including a Hanukya, and the photo album.

So yes, the joy of mutual recognition. And of familiarity. But there had also been a fear about our marriage. Nol's fear. As he himself had said, and as I knew—we had known each other for years by then—growing close to a woman who, like him, had survived the war, also spelled danger. The danger of getting close to his grief, close to the safely stored away box with its tightly-shut lid. The fear that the lid might be prized open. But love was stronger. We got married. We shared our lives. We wrote; he wrote his books, I mine. Yet even in his exhilarating novels, grief was kept at bay, and suffering a merciful joke. The *Holocaust* nothing more than a *holle kast (/hɔlɛ//kast/)*: a *hollow-closet*.

I remember a conversation about a just-written scene in which there was mention of one such hollow closet, wherein lurked something gruesome and threatening. The boy in the story had repeatedly overheard his parents whispering the words *holle kast*. That threat, the boy surmised, must be located on the mezzanine floor landing. This was where the staircase interrupted its own ascent and flattened out to create a small plateau, before resuming its course up to the second floor. And right there, on that little plateau was a hermetically sealed door, behind which was the *holle kast* with its gruesome content. It goes without saying that this locked door filled the boy with terror.

I said: Help the reader a bit, leave some crumbs, make it a little easier. This way, you won't be understood.

Nol refused.

I pleaded. Such a shame, such a beautiful metaphor.

He stuck to his guns: The reader will just have to figure it out for themself. I have.'

And so, the 'hollow closet' remained, unexplained.

Recognition, even though I was reunited with my mother, who returned from Auschwitz, and Nol remained with his "hiding family". The joy and melancholia of mutual recognition, recognition of the endless variations on the same theme, the Holocaust.

Nol taught me that every grief is the worst grief.

For Nol, the Jewish people were the People of the Book, of the Word. Not of land or flag or country. Words and even letters were sacred to him. You didn't throw those away. Ever. I still keep a drawer stuffed with scraps of paper torn out of notebooks or from notepads, sometimes scribbled on with only a single word or a single sentence, a thought, a line of poetry crossed out. He loved the gentle, wise, humorous People of the Word.

Rafael Baroch seems to align with the thoughts and feelings of my husband. Influenced by the philosophy of Emmanuel Levinas, a Jewish philosopher, he wrote in newspaper *Trouw* on 29 December 2023 that the true tragedy of the Israeli-Palestinian conflict lies not only in its physical destruction, but also in the loss of ethical values. The conflict between Israel and Hamas, he writes, is more than a struggle for land or power; it is a struggle for essence, for humanity and ethics. As a result, Israel seems to have lost a part of its own Jewish tradition, its ethical responsibility for the Other, and thereby a part of its identity.

V

Author Benjamin Moser went one step further, articulating my deepest feelings, when he wrote in in the Dutch National newspaper *Trouw*, on 16 December 2023, that 'Jews, especially Jews, should feel empathy with the Palestinian people.'

Moser so relentlessly condemned Israel's politics in his article that it pained me to read his statements. Because they are true. There it is again, I thought, that unwanted but apparently inevitable intertwining of being a Jew in the *galuth*—the Jewish diaspora— and being a Jew in Israel. An intertwining that makes me feel responsible for what is happening there, an unreasonable, unjust thought, I know. But knowing doesn't help free me from that entanglement.

The inescapable intertwining of being a Jew outside of Israel also means that atrocities—yes, atrocities— committed by Israeli, Jewish settlers on the West Bank, by Israeli Jewish guards of Palestinian prisoners in Israeli jails—which are regularly reported in *Haaretz*—cause a sense of outrage in me, to the point of almost not being able to read what is written.

Moser's article also hurts because it is not only Israel that is guilty. Hamas deliberately chose not to let Gaza flourish and prosper, deliberately chose not to prioritise the welfare of its citizens, but instead to oppress them. Hamas chose to engage in a fanatical religious-political struggle to wipe Israel off the map.

A religious struggle. By now, could it not be argued that the Netanyahu government—advocating a Greater Biblical Israel and condoning the reprehensible and dangerous acts of hundreds of thousands of settlers, is equally waging a religious war?

Israeli historian Moshe Zimmermann says (and I paraphrase): The story of a Greater Israel with its settlements is the story of a society held hostage to Biblical romanticism that will plunge the entire community into the abyss.

VI

The reason the statement, 'Jews, especially Jews, should feel empathy with the Palestinian people,' affects me so much might be best explained if I share two memories of me as a young girl.

It was the early 1950s. I was nine or ten, eleven at most. It was evening and my stepfather was out. We—my new sister, brother and I—were used to this. But once in a while my mother would go out after dark as well. Apparently, I was big enough to look after my much younger brother and sister.

My little brother, sister and I slept together in the children's bedroom. After our mother had tucked us in and promised to be back home soon, after I had refused to let go of my arms around her neck, and finally had let go, and I had seen her leave the dim room, heard the door close, then the door to our floor. After I had heard her footsteps going down the stairs and she slammed the outer door shut, I lay in bed, frozen with fear. After what seemed like an eternity, I sat upright, threw off the covers, and crept out of bed. I softly closed the nursery door behind me, walked through the hallway, past the door she had disappeared behind, walked through the living room to the window, and crawled under the curtains to look outside. To see people walking on the street, people acting as if nothing was wrong and the world had not ceased to exist. I kept looking, seeking reassurance in vain from the few cars that passed by, from cyclists, a pedestrian. The streetlights were on, outside life seemed to go on as usual, but inside it had come to a standstill and a child was dying of fear of losing her mother forever.

In my memory, I had to babysit dozens of times, but when I asked my mother about it later, she swore that it had happened rarely.

***

A winter's day. It had been freezing for days, the canal behind our house had been covered with a thick layer of ice. I was eight, nine, or maybe ten years old, and on my way home from school. I was walking along the canal. By myself. In my memory there was no one else on the street. The thick layer of ice that had covered the water on my way to school that morning, I could see, had broken into pieces. A boat must have come through. Countless ice floes shimmered and swayed on the water. It looked so tempting; you could just jump from one floe to another. Cautiously, I shuffled down the steep embankment, stepped on to the first ice floe, from there on to a second, a third. It was so easy. The floes were not far apart, the black water glistening in between, and I danced from one floe to another, arms spread wide. Until my dance was brusquely interrupted by a man's voice hollering at me: 'You! Get off the ice!' I looked up. At the top of the slope stood a big man with a red face. Startled, I jumped back on to land and clambered up. 'Go back to your mother, you!' the man shouted, and I started running, running, running.

Why do I remember this event? Because of my bewilderment. How on earth, I wondered, as I ran, did this strange man know my mother was still alive?

The Holocaust, the Shoah, was my frame of reference. The years of the Shoah meant danger. Danger was the Shoah. This was the reason why I often failed to recognise the danger around me. Yes, I knew how to cross the street. Look first to the left, then to the right. Don't accept sweets from strangers. But danger? That was something from back then, from the war. And the war was over, after all.

My essay, 'Reflections from an Expert', in the recently published anthology on the war and Israel and Gaza, *Wie over vrede spreekt, heeft moed (It Takes Courage to Talk About Peace)*, examines a life lived with trauma and growing up among adults carrying trauma. Trauma as a result of World War II.

Jews, especially Jews, should feel empathy with the Palestinian people.

VII

I was separated from my parents when I was two and a half years old. On that day in April 1944, Dutch policemen who were collaborators, on the orders of the Sicherheitsdienst in The Hague, forced their way into the house where my parents and I were in hiding. Due to a series of mistakes, I was not taken with my parents to Scheveningen prison, and from there to Westerbork, and from there to Auschwitz, as they were, but remained behind with my 'hiding family'. By the time the police-collaborators had realised their mistake and returned for me that evening, the Resistance had already moved me to another location.

I must have suppressed memories of the arrest. I do remember the following day. I was lying in an unfamiliar bed; two women were sitting at the foot of the bed looking at me. I didn't know who they were. The curtains had been pushed open, and it was broad daylight. And yet I was lying in bed. I must have come down with something.

My mother survived Auschwitz; my father did not. In June 1945, my mother and I were reunited. And I turned into a child who hung on to her skirts, a child who didn't want to play outside, a child who was sick a lot, a child who didn't want to eat, a child paralysed by fear when her mother went out for the evening, certain that her mother would never return.

This is exactly what Benjamin Moser is referring to. Jews, especially Jews, should feel empathy for the suffering of the civilian population in Gaza. After all, they know what it means to have no parents, like Nol, and like far too many children of the Holocaust, of the Shoah. Jews in particular should reject violence and look for any other means to bring security and peace. Because they do not want others to suffer as they and their families suffered. And often still suffer. Because they know what suffering is.

This is also why my wish is so self-evident: no child should have to endure these fears, barefoot and alone at the windows at night. Not anywhere. And I know at the same time that there are countless children in Gaza right now, every day, who have to grow up without fathers, without mothers, forever separated from them. And there are Israeli children, forever separated from their mothers and fathers, or from one of them. That is the reason why I am against this war.

Besides, I cannot believe in violence as a solution to this maddening conflict. Should Hamas be eliminated by the Israeli army, a new, even more extremist terror group will emerge. As it did in the wake of the US interventions after 9/11. The continued bombing by the Israeli government and Hamas will further split the world into For and Against. Into Black and White. Into a world of hatred, revenge and resentment. Into a world of antisemitism and Islamophobia. The way out of this nightmarish conflict will disappear even further out of sight. So too will the vision of a Palestinian state coexisting peacefully and in mutual respect with Israel.

And what of Israel's right to defend itself? Of course, but not in this way. As journalist and author Hella Rottenberg and I argued in an opinion piece in the newspaper *De Volkskrant* on 8 November 2023, the conflict should have been referred to the diplomatic arena from the start. At best, the hostages would have been released and tens of thousands of civilian casualties would have been avoided.

People do not learn from history. People do not become better people, more responsible people, nor more benign when they have been hated and persecuted, nor when their loved ones have been murdered. Even though there will always be exceptions. Maybe people do learn from history and it is bad people who have the most power?

VIII

I thank the Lord in Whom I do not believe (I believe) that my mother does not have to live through this war. My mother, who time and again, no matter how hard it was for her, testified in public to what had happened in the concentration camps and extermination camps. Testified to the murder of the Jews and Sinti and Roma so that it would never happen again. Testified to this unprecedented murder, conceived of and carried out in a cold, mechanical way on an industrial scale across more than sixteen hundred concentration camps, labour camps and extermination camps strategically located across Germany, Poland, Austria, France and the Netherlands, with the sole purpose of exploiting and killing people as slaves. Without anyone coming to the aid of the victims. Even the train tracks to the extermination camps were never bombed.

My mother testified to the gas chambers, to the gassing trucks, to the hundreds of thousands of Jews who were first forced to dig their own graves and strip naked, before they were shot by German firing squads, as in Babi Yar, not far from Kyiv.

> Come visit me at night with rhymes,
> of how the war at last was buried deep,
> repeat these lines a hundred times
> and each and every time I shall weep

poet Leo Vroman wrote about the genocide, the genocide of Jews.

The genocide committed by the Nazis was eagerly and methodically supported by countless European collaborators. Collaborators like the policemen who arrested my parents and later returned for me in vain. Collaborators in all German-occupied territories, without whose help the implementation of the genocide would not have been possible. Denmark was an exception, however. The Danes arranged safe passage for its relatively small Jewish community by boat to safe and neutral Sweden. The Germans, it seems, turned a blind eye to this, not out of compassion, obviously, but to get the benefit of raw materials from Sweden as a reward. And agricultural products from Danish soil, which were mainly transported to Germany. But still, Danish

Jews, all but a dozen or so, would safely return to their homeland.

And Bulgaria was an exception, though unfairly unacknowledged. There, many heeded King Boris of Bulgaria's call for Jews, at least Jewish women and children, to be taken to safety in mountain villages. Peasant families took Jewish women and children into their homes. Jewish men were put to work, but they too survived. Not a single Bulgarian Jew came to harm as a result of the war. Non-Bulgarian Jews fared far less well: they were deported to neighbouring countries, where they faced certain death.

King Boris of Bulgaria did not flee his country, as the Dutch royal family fled and the Dutch government fled ours. And even from the safety of London, Queen Wilhelmina and her government failed to call on the Dutch to do everything in their power to save their Jewish compatriots. In my most recently published novel, *Het verdriet van de vrede/The Sorrow of Peace*, I have Roza, one of the protagonists, sigh: 'Just imagine, Judit, if Queen Wilhelmina had called on the Dutch people from England to protect their Jewish neighbours, can you imagine if she had? If she had said, "Rescue your Jewish neighbours! Keep them out of German hands," what if, what if ...'

intermezzo

Once, Eastern Europe was dotted with shtetls—small villages where Jews lived. They spoke their own language, Yiddish. They had their own rich culture of musicians, writers and poets. I will name a few: Miryam Ullinover, Sholem Aleichem, S. Ansky (Schloyme Zanvl Rappoport), Abraham Sutzkever. And they had their own theatrical tradition. Also famous was Der Bund, founded in 1897. A Jewish socialist movement that did not see Palestine as a Jewish homeland, but advocated a two-state solution with equal rights for the Jewish and Arab-Palestinian populations. Der Bund showed its respect for other cultures through art and education.

Nothing was left of this culture after World War II, absolutely nothing. Even Jewish graves had been destroyed, gravestones ripped out of the ground, turned over and used for the construction of roads. Or smashed to pieces. A people, its culture and its language, wiped out. From all over Europe. Also, from the Netherlands. In our Netherlands, where more than seventy-five percent of the Jewish population was killed. And with them, their culture.

IX

My mother and her new husband taught us children to be human first and foremost. Secondly, Jewish. Being Jewish was considered secondary to being human. Being a good person was the key to her and my stepfather's upbringing.

Was it really secondary, or did our Jewishness, in spite of everything, seep through the cracks, much like the grief that seeped from the small box hidden under my husband's skin. Did our Jewishness seep into our very being, whether we liked it or not. And what did being Jewish mean without synagogue attendance, without prayers, without commandments and prohibitions and virtually without Jewish holidays and Jewish dietary laws. Did it make us less Jewish. Were we Holocaust Jews, branded and bound by The Great Jewish Suffering, as I reflect now. Not comforted, not consoled by the festive Jewish holidays, not singing around tables set with starched white tablecloths with burning Shabbat candles in their candlesticks. No solace in these age-old rituals. The support we had to live without, as human children drenched in Jewishness. Yet with the *neshama*, the Jewish soul, which was present nevertheless. I did not add question marks to the end of these sentences. Question marks would be inappropriate. These are musings, possibilities, uncertainties. Answers do not fit, certainly not ready-made ones.

Being different and not actually allowed to feel that fully; after all, we were human among humans. Still, we were different. Our food was different. People from other countries came to our house, among them our mother's French friends from Auschwitz. Without each other—and a lot of luck—they would not have survived the concentration camp. We spoke Yiddish at home; French, English, and German as well. Being different, and not being allowed to fully experience and acknowledge this, after all, we are all human. In many ways, it was a valuable and beautiful life lesson. For us, the road was not mapped out. For us, the path was not paved. Each of us had to find their own way.

Did this educational message from my youth influence my criticism of Israel's politics? Yes, I think it contributed to it. People are people first and foremost.

Then Jewish, or Hindu, or Sinti or of any faith. Being human is what connects us. Should connect us. This was my mother's view, strengthened by her suffering in Auschwitz. Strengthened during the death march through icy Poland and East Germany in the winter of 1945, driven forward by the Nazis. Finally arriving, exhausted and starving, at Groß-Rosen concentration camp, where she was saved in the nick of time by the Red Army, then still our allies. Exhausted and emaciated. This view was shared by my dear stepfather, a resistance fighter who had spent three years in concentration camps.

This is what was instilled in us: you shouldn't let another person suffer because they belong to a different people, or to a different race, or professes a different faith. A truth imprinted on our children's hearts. A truth like a rock.

Is it because of that, I think, that when I hear arguments from others who plead for a better understanding of Israel's war policy, passionate, sincere arguments, that they cannot convince me?

No, I say. No. I keep saying no to what is happening there in Gaza.

It can't happen.

It shouldn't happen.

Again and again, it's what I return to. Again and again, I am drawn to that rock-shaped foundation of humanity, towering above the seas of arguments and opinions. I am pushed towards it, planted on top of it and fused with it.

Sometimes I wish I could mindlessly add my voice to the opinions of those who passionately defend Israel's attack on Gaza. And believe in the version of historical facts and events they present so fervently. Let myself be rocked into that shared sleep. Alas, I can't. I don't really have doubts. It's more like a desire to drift along in my tribe's comfort zone, wanting to be one with them, uniting under their banner and no longer having to think for myself or feel lonely. But I can't go along with the rhetoric of righteous revenge. **Because What Israel Is Doing Now, It Should Not.** In Gaza. And in the occupied West Bank. Not in our name. Our Jewish name. Not in my Jewish name.

X

Months have passed since the war started. Months have passed since the massacre, rapes, and hostage-taking by Hamas. The people of Israel are still in a state of shock. For months, bombs have been falling on Gaza, obliterating one residential block after another as the population searches for safe havens that are not there. And the death toll continues to rise alarmingly. In Israel, the population is fleeing into its shelters. Shelters that the Hamas government failed to provide for its Gaza population. Instead, money was used to construct a network of tunnels, purchase weapons, and build villas in Qatar, where the Hamas political leadership lives safely, surrounded by luxury. On money stolen from its citizens.

In their struggle to win the sympathy of the world, both Hamas and Israel wield the terms 'genocide', 'Holocaust' or 'Shoah' indiscriminately. Unhindered by any knowledge, or with contempt for the facts, and always with the goal of damaging the other with words.

The misuse of these concepts is diametrically opposed to the dream of the two journalists Ahmed Alnaouq and Yuval Abraham. Just as the absence of consultation and the misuse of historical facts are diametrically opposed to the Across the Wall project. Across the Wall, that project aimed at transcending the hostility between the people of Gaza and that of Israel.

On December 12, 2023, the newspaper *NRC* published an interview with Marileen Dogterom. As president of the Royal Netherlands Academy of Arts and Sciences (KNAW), Dogterom had received a petition on Gaza and Israel with a request to sign it. Dozens of employees of several KNAW-affiliated institutes had already signed it. The petition's signatories were urging her to speak out against Israel's 'genocide' of the inhabitants of Gaza. And they used the word 'genocide' with the convenience of the uninformed.

For his part, the Israeli ambassador to the United Nations wielded the word Holocaust in a similarly ignorant fashion. He pinned that hateful yellow star—like the one on my husband's boyhood jacket—to the lapel of his jacket. His staff then copied the bizarre gesture. They sat there, pretending they couldn't defend themselves. As if nothing had changed when Israel was founded in 1948. There they sat, pretending they were still defenceless victims. As if it was still the same as when Jews—for centuries—were driven from their homes, their shtetl, or evicted from the land where they had sometimes lived for generations without anyone bothering about them. Unless they had been murdered already. Victims of centuries-long antisemitism, of endlessly repeated pogroms, culminating in the Holocaust. When there was no one to ask for help. And the whole world looked the other way. Even, as I have already said, the railway tracks leading to the extermination camps, even those were not bombed by the Allies, so that the transportations to death could continue calmly, running like clockwork.

The Israeli ambassador and his staff live in a country with a large and strong army. That army had been largely deployed by the Netanyahu government at the time of the Hamas massacre to protect colonists on the West Bank so that they could go about their vile business.

Immediately after the Six-Day War in 1967, Yeshayahu Leibowitz, then a professor at the University of Jerusalem, was one of the first to warn against the occupation of the West Bank. He was particularly concerned about the dehumanising effect it would have on the Palestinian victims. And on the occupiers, themselves.

An outgrowth of that ongoing policy of occupation—I cannot help but mention it here—is the blatantly genocidal comments made by several of Netanyahu's ministers. Perhaps it's better described the other way round. It was successive Netanyahu governments who created the occupation policy—and, therefore, caused the alarming growth in settler numbers—that led to these comments. These ministers were voted into power by an electorate whose fears were fuelled by the populist rhetoric of those successive right-wing governments.

A truly deplorable state of affairs that has its roots in the Six-Day War, when, for a variety of reasons, the West Bank was not returned to the Palestinians. With catastrophic consequences for the Palestinian population, and, ultimately, for Israel itself.

Since then, many others have joined Yeshayahu Leibowitz in warning against that occupation. Among them David Grossman, the Israeli author and national moral compass. Grossman has been opposed to the West Bank occupation his entire life. Just like the historian Moshe Zimmermann, who was taken to court several times for criticising Israeli policy.

Back to Marileen Dogterom, president of KNAW. Should she have signed the petition demanding an end to the genocide by Israel? Instead of coming prepared and explaining what genocide entails, she invoked the fact that her organisation is not a political organisation. As if the definition of genocide would not be easy to look up. As if one is unable to read when that is momentarily not so convenient. As if that term should be watered down at all costs. Misused. Stripped of its substance. So that people—finally—can say to us Jews: 'You are just as bad as the Nazis, you are doing exactly the same.' Making it easier to brush away the guilt about the widespread collaboration with the Nazis during World War II, as well as the pervasive indifference (except for those who joined the Resistance) as Jews were being deported.

The KNAW president defended herself purely on the grounds that the academy is not a political organisation. But it is, however, a scientific institute. The institute's representatives should feel obligated to do some research first. They would quickly learn that the Polish-Jewish lawyer Raphael Lemkin was the first to coin the term *genocide* to describe the extermination of the Jews by the Nazis. British Historian and author Philippe Sands described Lemkin's long struggle to get the term genocide accepted in his book *East West Street*, an impressive examination of Lemkin's struggle for justice. It was only after World War II, when Lemkin worked for the International Military Tribunal, commonly known as the Nuremberg trials, that the definition of genocide was accepted. Lemkin was attached to the legal team of Robert H. Jackson, the chief prosecutor. Once the term's legal definition had been accepted, the judiciary could use the concept of genocide when prosecuting atrocities committed by the Nazis.

Genocide is not new. Genocide was committed—even before the genocide of Jews, Sinti and Roma—against the Armenian people, a Christian people living in the Muslim world. A tragedy that deeply affected and deeply troubled Raphael Lemkin. There was no word with which to describe what had taken place there. The concept of genocide was not yet to be found in any international jurisprudence.

The genocide of Armenians took place at the time of the First World War. Turks forced the Armenians out of their homes, drove them in endless columns deep into the Syrian desert for weeks on end, where they were abandoned and left to die from thirst and exhaustion. It cost the lives of an estimated one to one-and-a-half million Armenians. Franz Werfel wrote about it, in his unforgettable 1933 novel *Forty Days of the Musa Dagh*.

Genocide was only recently committed against the Yazidis by IS. And years before that in Cambodia. There, the entire urban population and intelligentsia were massacred during the terror of the Khmer Rouge. Minutely chronicled by the then 12-year-old girl Buth Keo. Together with a niece, Keo was the only survivor of her large family, and was adopted by French parents. Natalia Ginzburg translated her account from French into Italian as *Il racconto di Peuw bambina Cambogiana* (later published in English under the title *The Stones Cry Out*), referring to Keo in her foreword as the "the Cambodian Anne Frank".

At this very moment, the Chinese government is committing genocide against the Uyghurs, against their culture and their language. The Uyghur and Tibetans have been living under Han-Chinese occupation for years.

I am aware that this list of genocides is far from exhaustive.

XI

Genocide, yet again misunderstood.

In an emotional hearing before a Congressional committee in Washington, Harvard University president Dr Claudine Gay was asked to unconditionally reject and condemn the call for genocide against Jews—a call that had apparently resounded through the university, sending Jewish students into fear and panic. To unconditionally reject or to approve. So, a simple yes or no.

Gay avoided answering the question at her hearing in Washington. Instead, she replied "that it depended on the context, that it depended on whether it was just words or if they led to actions". The actions she would disapprove of.

Claudine Gay was not the only one giving testimony. There were two other presidents of equally renowned universities sitting next to her. They, too, evaded committee chair Elise Stefanik's question as to whether Claudine Gay and the two other chairs approved or disapproved of the call for genocide of Jews. Significantly, none of the three actually denied that there had been calls for genocide.

Journalist Ian Buruma argued in newspaper *NRC* on 5 January 2024 that if the same question had been asked about Black people, there wouldn't have been an issue of 'context'. But this wasn't about Black people, it was about Jews, whose lives carry the generational scars of genocide. Ian Buruma argued that Gay fell into a trap, as Stefanik deliberately made no distinction between, on the one hand, students on campus chanting 'intifada', which means 'uprising' in Arabic, and, on the other hand, calls for genocide against Jews. Chanting 'intifada' is of a completely different order than calls for a genocide. Calls for genocide, any genocide, should always be met with a 'no, we will not now, not ever, accept that'. Even if there are 'intifada' chants. Even when there is no context.

Setting a trap for Claudine Gay to walk into, as Ian Buruma noted? Watching the video of that deliberate interrogation by Stefanik, one has to conclude that her attitude could be perceived as intimidating—emotional, even. That may have played a role. But it obviously does not change the fact that calling for genocide is a serious and dangerous crime and always unacceptable.

There is a further aspect to this. I assume that Claudine Gay is a highly intelligent woman. And, also, that she has read a thing or two, and holds such a high and responsible position for a reason. In that position, I think she should know, it should have been ingrained in her, that wars never just fall from the sky (just as the terrorist organisation Hamas did not fall out of the sky), but that wars always start with words. Words misused to damage people, to dehumanise them, to achieve one's own ends, as has been happening for years; even in The Netherlands, by what is currently the largest political party. Claudine Gay should know the importance of using words and terms with integrity, honesty and sincerity: to preserve democracy, to preserve the rule of law.

Did she not know her history? Did she not know, to give an example, of the existence of Mille Collines, the Rwandan radio station that for months on end in 1994 used certain words to call on the Hutus to kill the Tutsi population? In those radio broadcasts, Tutsis were repeatedly referred to as 'cockroaches' and 'vermin'.

A dehumanising tactic. Pertinently, the radio station used the word 'work' when describing, and inciting, the murder of Tutsis. Eventually, whipped up and indoctrinated by the words used on radio station Mille Collines, the Hutu population began to massacre their neighbours. A gruesome, weeks-long massacre that resulted in more than five hundred thousand deaths.

The genocide of the Tutsis was mobilised by words.

Did Claudine Gay perhaps not know that in the period directly preceding World War II the Nazis referred to Jews as 'cockroaches'? And referred to themselves as 'Herrenvolk' and 'Übermenschen'? That they considered people living in the Slavic countries as merely 'Untermenschen'? That Jews were likewise dehumanised with that word, even though, in the eyes of the Nazis, Jews were even less than 'Untermenschen'. While children were poisoned with words in the years of rising fascism and during the ensuing war. From one day to the next, these children no longer wanted to play with their Jewish friends.

In Yugoslavia, where Bosnians, Croats, Serbs and Montenegrins had lived peacefully side by side and in friendship for decades, and sometimes married each other, that harmony came to an abrupt end with the death of President Tito. The language of nationalism was unleashed. The 'us' and the 'them'. Resulting in tens of thousands of deaths.

I am aware that my list is far from complete.

On 4 January 2024 *NRC*'s headline was: 'Why Harvard's Rector Resigned'. The full-page article reports extensively on Claudine Gay's alleged plagiarism. Or the insufficient source citation, as others claim. A paltry handful of sentences are devoted to her refusal to respond with a clear 'yes' or 'no' to the question of whether or not threats of genocide against Jews should be rejected. Without going further into what the definition of genocide is.

XII

Misuse of words, it is as old as mankind. And to this day, it goes on and on; using words to manipulate history for one's own gain. As was on display on the national news on 27 November 2023 when, during his address of Parliament, without batting an eyelid, President Recep Erdoğan of Turkey compared Netanyahu to Hitler. This was a prime example of clear anti-Jewish/Israeli language being used in order to present oneself as pro-Palestinian. Erdoğan hopes this deliberate, historically inaccurate comparison will increase his chances of a reelection victory.

Another example. Masha Gessen, the prominent Russian-American journalist and philosopher, *and* Jewish, compared Gaza to the Jewish ghettos in Nazi-occupied Europe during World War II in a recently published essay.

And yes, here we go again.

Life for Gazans is now hell on earth. With the whole world watching on. (Except for the people of Israel, most of whom are exhausted and asleep when these images of hell are aired, if they are aired at all.)

The world remained silent about the fate of the Jews trapped in ghettos during World War II. This way, the Nazis could go about their business undisturbed. And no trucks— however few—came with food and medicine to relieve the very worst needs. There were no UN relief troops. The Red Cross was conspicuous by its absence. Journalists did not report on what was happening in the ghettos for the whole world to see and take action. Away from the eyes of the world, Jews in the ghettos, Jewish men, women and children, if they had not already died from hunger or exhaustion after only a few months, were herded onto trains that took them away to extermination camps to be gassed immediately. *But now, in May 2025, I acknowledge with a heavy heart that Masha Gessen's comparison of Gaza to the ghettos comes close to this truth.*

Without detracting from what I noted above, I nevertheless feel I must mention here, and with a heavy heart, that journalists in Gaza—those who reported on the bombings, the dead and wounded, and the hunger—lost their lives in shockingly large numbers. Journalists from Gaza who never knew press freedom under Hamas.

And with a heavy heart, I should mention that the Netanyahu government has done everything it can to make the hell in Gaza even more intolerable. By killing journalists, bombing water pipes and hospitals, and even tent camps. This without any leniency towards the civilian population. Hamas, sadly, has no clemency with its own civilian population either.

As I said, Nol taught me that every grief is the worst grief. It makes no difference to the victim if their suffering was the result of genocide or revenge on a mass scale. One's own suffering is not perceived as more or less.

But that is no excuse for using concepts such as genocide carelessly. Or Holocaust or Shoah.

Raphäel Lemkin, he who fought for the legal acceptance of the term genocide, who fought for justice, he would be turning in his grave, as they say, had he known how the term genocide currently is being peddled for the sake of being in the right, for the sympathy of the world.

This is the definition of genocide:

Genocide is a crime committed with the intent to destroy a national, ethic, racial or religious group, in whole or in part. The word genocide may be used if the intention, the goal, is to eradicate all or most of the aforementioned populations.

Whether the term genocide is used correctly concerning Gaza is a matter for the International Court of Justice to decide.

But the situation is already catastrophic.

XIII

Not just Israel and Hamas are now more than ever sworn enemies. The conflict is polarising worldwide. Including in my own country, in the city where I live. The majority of the population has rallied behind the Palestinians, and sometimes even Hamas, with a great emotion that often lacks nuance. This includes people who don't belong to the Palestinian people, who aren't Muslim and who have no connection to Jews.

An unfortunate outcome of the massive support for the Palestinian cause: the flaring up of antisemitism. In particular on American campuses where Jewish students live in fear and try to conceal their identity, without the necessary support from the leadership of those Universities. Like at Harvard University, where there were calls for genocide against Jews.

Antisemitism stems from a legacy of centuries-old prejudices, according to historian Moshe Zimmermann.

But since the founding of the Jewish state, criticism of Israel and antisemitism have become increasingly interchangeable. Antisemites exploit this interchangeability by masking their attacks behind, between and under criticism of Israel. In the aftermath of October 7, they feel further empowered and protected. As does the Netanyahu government, dismissing justified criticism of Israel as antisemitism.

My eldest son's daughter, a veterinary student, asked me, 'But why does everyone immediately have to take sides?'

She appears to feel alone, in this respect, among her housemates and fellow students. I tell her that standing squarely behind the Palestinians, or indeed behind Israel, is easier than being brave enough to contemplate the complex situation and act accordingly. It will help you, I tell her, to get rid of a sense of powerlessness. Turning powerlessness into anger: formulating cut-and-dry opinions, waving your fist and shouting slogans at demonstrations, one way or the other, I tell her, these are things that offer immediate relief.

She understands.

I am proud of my granddaughter, proud of her independent mind, and I tell her so. It will not make life easier for her, I fear. And I also think of my husband, Nol. He liked to wish family and friends 'a dose of curiosity' for their birthday. Curiosity about other opinions and about knowledge. Curiosity, Nol's wish implied, was and is the opposite taking a rigid stance.

XIV

Across the globe, people have instinctively connected with the Palestinian suffering, while the suffering of others, often also Muslim communities living in equally wretched conditions, has not mobilised people in anywhere near equal measure, and there is hardly anyone who shows concern or cares about their plight. Bart Wallet, professor of Jewish history, wrote an insightful essay on this topic in *De Groene Amsterdammer* on 16 November 2023.

What it comes down to, says Bart Wallet, and I paraphrase: Europeans have a special and close bond with Israel. Their culture is anchored in the Christianity that originated there. Bart Wallet reminds us of the birth of Jesus. Reminds us of Bethlehem. Of the crusades. And explains that the Western world feels more involved in what happens there for that reason. As if for them, he says, God is 'a bit closer' in Jerusalem.

For the Muslims expelled from their own country by Myanmar, languishing for years in tents in poverty-stricken Bangladesh, that tragedy feels distant. Nor do people here take to the streets to protest against the genocide of the Yazidis by IS. Nor were there demonstrations when Assad, aided by Putin, his ally in ultimate evil, bombed his own people out of Syria. Not even after decades of terrorising and torturing his own Syrian citizens.

And again, the list is far from complete.

XV

Gideon Levy, an equally inspired and left-wing Israeli journalist, argued in an interview in *The Volkskrant* on 8 December 2023 that the Dutch are probably better informed about Palestinian suffering in Gaza than the Israelis. And better informed about Palestinian suffering on the West Bank. That observation is supported by my nephew writing from Haifa: images of Gaza, he writes, are occasionally shown very late at night.

This is partly why I walk on eggshells when I'm in touch with my family in Israel. These dear, warm, caring people who demonstrated continuously for nine months against the Netanyahu government, against its intention to cripple the Supreme Court and subsequently its democracy; gentle folk, who were in friendly contact with Palestinians; when we talk about the conflict, I weigh my words carefully.

I feel this too with my niece, Maja, who lives in a kibbutz not far from Gaza. She compiled a cookbook together with Druze women. And Rivka, who works at an insemination clinic and 'makes babies', as she herself describes it. Jewish babies as well as Palestinian babies. Open-minded women, both. Yet I don't tell them what I think about the war. I am afraid of losing them—at least temporarily—and especially afraid of hurting them now that they themselves live in fear for their children in the army, and in fear of attacks. Feeling isolated and misunderstood in their small country on the Mediterranean, surrounded by enemies. Horrified as they were, after October 7. Because everyone knows someone who was a victim of Hamas or who was taken hostage by them. Horrified also by the daily death toll. And in the painful realisation, as David Grossman puts it (I paraphrase), that they live in a constant state of tension and preparedness for war. With the existential doubt as to whether they will ever live a free life; free from terror and fear, stable and protected. A life that constitutes a home.

Seen in that light, it is understandable that my family has at this time no emotional space for the suffering of the civilian population in Gaza, although of course I regret this. And on top of that, as Gideon Levy writes, they are denied information about the suffering of Palestinians in Gaza.

A report in newspaper *Haaretz* on 31 December 2023 confirms this:

> "The Israeli media is concealing the scale of destruction in Gaza: the number of dead, the true extent of the humanitarian disaster. The little information that does trickle through from foreign sources is distrusted by the population or seen as hostile propaganda against Israel".

What about the other side? In an interview with *The Sun*, Egyptian writer Dalia Ziada says that the Arab world is unaware of what took place in Israel on 7 October.

intermezzo

And then the Israeli army killed three Israeli hostages. The hostages had crawled out of the Hamas tunnels, bare-chested, waving white rags. Bare-chested to signal they were not wearing a bomb belt. Defenceless. Three young men who had been held captive for months by Hamas terrorists. For months, they had been cut off from sun and light and air, held captive in the kilometre-long tunnels. They had managed to escape their guards. How they had managed to do so, no one will ever know. They had made it out of the tunnels; for the first time in months, their skin felt fresh air; for the first time in months, they inhaled the fresh air, as they waved white rags of surrender. Arms held high.

So great was the Israeli soldiers' fear, so great their distrust, tensions had run so high, and besides: the Israeli young men held hostage were indistinguishable from Palestinian young men. They looked alike, just like the journalist from Gaza and the journalist from Israel, the two once-inspired friends who shared the same dreams, had looked alike. Just as in the eyes of the café-goers they might have been mistaken for brothers, or cousins, when they sat (in my imagination) opposite each other in that café, forging their plans for peace.

The three hostages were shot dead.

I read in *Haaretz* about the mother of one of the escaped hostages. The thought that her child, if only for a moment, had felt fresh air, seen the sky, was her only consolation.

XVI

An excerpt from a letter to my nephew Uri in Haifa, Israel:

To do justice
the Israelis should not only look inwards
they should also look outwards, to see what the world outside of Israel sees and
what they do not get to see.
The rest of the world only sees a glimpse of Israel's suffering.
Mainly, what we get to see is the suffering in Gaza, on a daily basis, on primetime TV, there is no escaping it.

This is what we are told every day:
people's homes are being destroyed in Gaza, they have no clean drinking water, no medicine, hardly any food, they are fleeing from the north to the south only to be bombed there too. We see their dead,
we see their wounded,
we see their children suffer, we see parents in mourning,

see children covered in blood, being carried by their fathers, uncles and cousins to ambulances in desperation. If there are any ambulances.

*Jews especially should not want
others to suffer as they themselves have had to suffer.
And the Israeli government should let its citizens know
what these images
are doing outside of Israel,
how they inflame anti-Semitism.
Because that's how it always goes.
They should not only think about a safe homeland for
Jews in Israel, they should also think about
the safety of Jews outside of Israel.
You are the only person in Israel I dare to write this to.
Please forgive me this cry for help.*

The letter is in response to his, and that of a colleague at the University of Haifa. First, my nephew's letter. He begins by confirming what I already understood. The suffering in Gaza is hardly shown in Israel, if at all. There are hardly any images on TV, and if they are, as the *Haaretz* journalist Gideon Levy pointed out, it's very late at night. So no, or hardly any images, only the written word. The focus is entirely on their own suffering.

"But you need to understand", my nephew wrote, *"that the news here follows a certain sense of priority that is quite different to the rest of the world. There are many complaints from abroad against Israel about this. Day in day out the news starts with listing the names of the fallen, showing their funerals, interviews with relatives, sometimes even with soldiers from their army units (many of these on the radio). It's constantly depressing. Then of course there is the hostage situation and discussion about the extremely complicated negotiations around that."*

He also forwards a letter from a colleague:

... In Tel Aviv, the younger generation of secular leftists [...] are now completely committed to eliminating Hamas whatever the cost [...] My daughters and their boyfriends tell me that they don't know a single (ex-)leftist person who didn't change their position after October 7th [...] Every young person knew people who were murdered, kidnapped, disappeared, or went through a life-threatening experience on October 7th [...] their political thinking has changed forever. If anything, they are more right-wing now regarding the Palestinians ... because the victims of the massacre were overwhelmingly party-going (ex-)peaceniks, left-wing kibbutzniks, and Bedouins, not religious people or secular supporters ... literally the same

people who were protesting against the law reforms in the months preceding October 7th— [...]. It is difficult to imagine that any leftist Israeli who talks to his or her children could maintain the same position after October 7th...

His letter shocked me to the core. How much it pained me that these young people and their parents, and with them the vast majority of the Israeli population, no longer has the emotional capacity to go looking for information beyond that which they are receiving from their own news outlets; to learn about what is unfolding in Gaza for themselves, to go on their own fact-finding expeditions. They have every freedom to do so. Unlike the citizens of Russia, who have little or no access to news reports from abroad, and for whom it is life-threatening to investigate on their own. But Israeli citizens seem convinced that they are well informed and, for this reason, apparently see no need to consult other sources.

Then I received the following joint message from my nieces, three sisters:

We are so sad,
every day we hear the
terrible stories about October 7th,

*but the UN, women's organisations, the Red Cross
are biased and anti-Semitic,
the proceedings in The Hague
is a stain on the western world, we cannot breathe,
we are worried about a war in the north,
we are worried about our existence here.
Our children are dying every day,
we are tired and our hearts are broken.*

Heart-wrenching, genuine grief. But grief has also blinded them to the other side of this bitter tale. To want to see it. Or to be able to see it. And even if a smattering of doubt was to surface, it would most likely be unconsciously kept at bay. Because the whole saga is unbearable.

Many questions arise. What needs to happen or change for the once left-wing hopeful youngsters and adults, like my family, to want and dare to see the other side of the argument once more? And to feel that wish. How might they bring down, or lift up, or park somewhere else to use a somewhat flat expression, that wall of self-protection erected from the debris of grief, fear and anger, and still be open to the suffering on the other side of that wall?

A new *Across the Wall* project, when that war is finally over? But that will not be nearly enough. So much more needs to be done. And should those once-leftist Israelis open themselves up to the Other, to those they see as the enemy, and realise that violence is not— never is— the answer, what must it be like for parents, grandparents, for families, to inevitably reach the maddening conclusion that their children on the frontline, their grandchildren, brothers and sisters, are sacrificing their lives for nothing.

XVII

Foreign Affairs, 8 December 2023. An article by Jessica Stern and Bessel van der Kolk. A shockingly insightful article. In a systematically responsible manner, it explains Hamas' extremely vicious attack, followed by Israel's disproportionate response. It validates the words of my nephew in Haifa and those of his university colleague. It makes clear why it is I walk on eggshells when I am in contact with my family in Israel. It shows how Palestinians under Hamas and Israelis under the extremist Netanyahu government blindly, and with eyes wide open, fell into the psychological trap laid out over many years by both sides, possibly without adequately foreseeing the consequences. The article substantiates the idea that violence offers no solution, no resolution. It does not bring peace any closer. Not now, not ever.

The authors are authorities in the field of knowledge and treatment of trauma. They write (I paraphrase) that every perpetrator of terrorism experiences themselves as a victim. Terrorism, the authors argue, is psychological warfare and therefore requires a deliberate psychological approach. The adage "hurt people, hurt people" holds true also for terrorists. And those who live in existential fear are more likely to dehumanise others. Hamas, for instance, will call Israelis 'infidels', for them the worst possible slur. While Israeli Defence Minister Yoav Gallant refers to members of Hamas as 'human beasts'. Both call the other 'Nazis'. This type of verbal dehumanisation paves the way for physical violence. Additionally, this shared legacy of trauma means Israelis and Palestinians are more susceptible when it comes to resorting to the use of *extreme* violence. And, so, a seemingly endless cycle of bloodshed continues.

Terrorists, the authors write, tend to challenge their enemy to a disproportionate response, as did Hamas on 7 October. They—the Hamas terrorists—hoped, first and foremost, to be seen as victims of the Israeli violence they provoked and thus win the sympathy of the world.

Hamas' second reason for provoking a disproportionately violent response from Israel is to create a new generation of radicalised people damaged by violence.

The sadistic massacre inflicted by Hamas on 7 October, the writers explain, has reopened the wounds of the Shoah for many Israelis. On the other side, the Israeli response has reignited the pain of the Nakba (Arabic for the Palestinian 'Catastrophe'), when the Palestinians were expelled from their land and the Jewish state was founded.

To be clear, the Nakba took place after the United Nations recognised the state of Israel. *After* neighbouring Arab countries invaded to wipe this new nation off the map. In April 1948, through an offensive— Plan Dalet— Israel tried to quickly capture as much land as possible from the Palestinians. The ensuing Arab-Israeli war was won by Israel. Hundreds of thousands of Palestinians were expelled. Hundreds of thousands fled in fear.

The mass expulsion of Jews from Arab states after the creation of the Jewish state is less well known. Expelled from countries where they had lived in relative peace for generations. Expelled without being allowed to take their possessions with them. Those numbers are a near match for the number of Palestinians expelled from the newly-created Israel.

We are locked in a traumatic and death-clinching embrace, say the *Foreign Affairs* contributors, an embrace in which Israelis and Gazans both— understandably— see themselves as the victim. And with what they feel as rightful, justified anger. As well as the desire for retaliation. Meanwhile, both vie for the world's sympathy.

For the good of both Israelis and Palestinians, Hamas will have to be removed from power, the authors conclude. This will not be achieved through intensive bombing. The best way to fight terrorists is to avoid civilian casualties, they write. Otherwise, the cycle of victimisation and violence will actually breed more terrorists. This cycle must be broken by pressure from outside. By the United States, Europe and the Arab countries, is the final conclusion of both authors.

XVIII

The authors of the *Foreign Affairs* article argue that the cycle of victimisation and violence must be broken by pressure from outside. To this I would add that it will also take pressure from within. Pressure from those Israelis who know how to break the chains of this cycle of violence and victimisation. Like the two journalists from Israel and Gaza. Like the Israeli journalist Gideon Levy. Like the writer David Grossman, who, I'll say it again, is Israel's moral compass. Like eighteen-year-old conscientious objector Tal Mitnick, who chose prison over fighting in Gaza. Like the dozen individuals pictured in a photograph in newspaper *Het Parool*, who stood silently demonstrating against the war, holding up placards illustrated with red, broken hearts. Like Meir Baruchin, the history teacher who was thrown into prison for five days for his criticism of Netanyahu's government's policies, temporarily suspended, and upon returning to his school was booed and berated by students. Like the recent, tentative criticism from (a few?) Israeli soldiers at the front. Like the recent peace demonstration on 19 January 2024 in Tel Aviv (attended by two thousand people, according to *Haaretz*); demonstrators who shouted, 'Peace from the river to the sea.'

Again, I am aware that my list is far from complete.

XIX

As I put the finishing touches on this essay, the violence continues. Talks are scheduled between the US and a handful of Arab states about ending the bombing and violence, conditional on the creation of a Palestinian state. Netanyahu continues to oppose ending the war; he continues to oppose the creation of a Palestinian state. Netanyahu, let it be known, rules with an iron fist. Peace would not only mark the beginning of the end of his political career, he would also in all likelihood face the prospect of a new career behind bars.

As I put the finishing touches on this essay, not only does Hamas pose a threat, but Hezbollah and the Houthis, backed by Iran, also pose a threat to Israel. The latter are targeting (for now just) Israel's northern borders. The residents of countless villages and kibbutzim in that region have already had to abandon their homes and their belongings. As have the inhabitants of villages on the other side of that border. More than one million people on the Rafah border are being trapped like rats. The threat of a Third World War continues to loom.

As I put the finishing touches to this essay, there's a storm brewing in the Netherlands over a lecture series about the Holocaust. Following pro-Palestinian pressure, this series, scheduled at the University of Applied Sciences, Utrecht, was cancelled, before this decision was subsequently reversed. Once again, the entwining of the Holocaust with the current war is glaringly evident. This entwining tarnishes the memory and history of the Holocaust. Not only that, it lays a thick blanket of fog over the conflict between Israel and Gaza. This makes reading testimonial literature on the Holocaust more necessary than ever. Let me mention the names of several great writers: Charlotte Delbo, Primo Levi, Tadeusz Borowski and Imre Kertész. Because it is only through reading these authors that you can sympathise and empathise, somewhat, with what took place. That is the power of literature.

I hope that by the time this essay is in bookshops, a prolonged ceasefire will be in effect, and that this, in turn, will lead to a permanent silencing of bullets, bombs and shells. And I hope a start will have been made on a viable peace plan that will rule out armed conflict between Israel and the Palestinians once and for all.

XX

After some hesitation, I shared the *Foreign Affairs* article with my niece, Mady—a psychotherapist—in Israel. And asked for her response. She read the article and replied: 'I need more time for this.'

I replied that I understood.

XXI

There is a Hasidic legend that is very dear to me. The legend tells of the thirty-six righteous, the Lamed Vav Tzadikim. It is for their sake alone that God does not let the world perish. The thirty-six righteous people carry all the sorrow and pain of the world in their hearts, without knowing, including themselves, who they are. When one of the righteous enters heaven, so the legend goes, they are so cold that God has to warm them with His own hands. On rare occasions, it will take Him more than a thousand years to do so.

Chaja Polak,
12 February 2024 / May 2025
Amsterdam

A Letter in the Night
Chaja Polak
Translated from the Dutch by Astrid Alben
Originally published as *Brief in de nacht – Gedachten over Israël en Gaza*
by Cossee (NL) March 2024. Published by arrangement
with Cossee International Agency.

This edition was first published in The United Kingdom in July 2025
by The New Menard Press

Copyright © 2024, 2025 Chaja Polak
Copyright © 2025 The New Menard Press / Astrid Alben

Author's photo Chaja Polak © Irwan Droog

Chaja Polak asserts the moral right to be identified as the author of this work in accordance with the Copyright, Designs and Patents Act 1988. A CIP catalogue record for this book is available from the British Library.

ISBN: 9781068680410

Thank you for buying an authorized copy of this book and for complying with copyright laws by not reproducing, scanning or distributing any part of it in any form without permission of the publisher and author. The New Menard Press supports copyright. Copyright fuels creativity, encourages diverse voices, promotes freedom of speech and creates a vibrant culture. You are supporting indie writers and publishers and allowing them to continue to make books together.

The editor and translator are responsible for the corrections
of the original text.

The translator gratefully acknowledges the support of
the Dutch Foundation for Literature.

N ederlands
letterenfonds
dutch foundation
for literature

Text editing by Elte Rauch / Alex Spears
Design by Martijn Dentant, Armée de Verre Bookdesign, Ghent, Belgium
Typeset in Martina Plantijn
Printed and bound in the UK by CMP Ltd.
www.thenewmenardpress.com